On the Tongue

by Jeff Mann

Arlington, Virginia

Published by Gival Press, an imprint of Gival Press, LLC.

For information please write:
Gival Press, LLC, P. O. Box 3812, Arlington, VA 22203.
Website: www.givalpress.com
Email: givalpress@yahoo.com

First edition ISBN 1-928589-35-9 (ISBN 13: 978-1-928589-35-8)
Library of Congress Control Number: 2006924427

Bookcover photo by Jack Slomovits.
Photo of Jeff Mann by John Ross.
Format and design by Ken Schellenberg.

ACKNOWLEDGMENTS

"Doom" appeared in *RFD* 27.4 (Spring 2003): 32.
"Magnolia" appeared in *RFD* 27.4 (Spring 2003): 32.
"Prisms" appeared in *RFD* 30.1 (Fall 2003): 35.
"One Definition of the Perfect Lover" appeared in *RFD* 29.1 (Fall 2002): inside front cover.
"Coconut Fried Pie" appeared in *RFD* 26.3 (Spring 2000): 38.
"Would-Be Husband Turns Whore" appeared in *Iris* 1.4 (Fall 1993): 54-55.
"Ghost and Vampire Tour, New Orleans" appeared in *Nox: A Journal of the Night 8* (Fall 2000): n.p.
"John's Apple Pie" appeared in *Appalachian Heritage* 31.2 (Spring 2003): 48-49.
"Downs" appeared in *The Burg and Other Poems*, edited by Anne Cheney (Lewiston, NY: Mellen Poetry Press, 1998).
"Holiness" and "Late May Mountain Gifts" appeared in *Queer Poetry* 3: n.p.
"Gray" and "Ice" appeared in *Shenandoah* 55.1 (Spring/Summer 2005): 36, 37.
"Return" appeared in *The Cream City Review.*
"Kilts" appeared in *Off the Rocks.*
"In Ireland" appeared in *Chiron Review.*
"The Ladies Mile Pub" appeared in *Kestrel.*

Advance Praise for *On the Tongue*

"*On the Tongue* is a poetry of sensuality, elemental as stone, wood and wind, outside of time and yet totally rooted in place. Jeff Mann is undoubtedly a modern incarnation of Pan and the Appalachians are his Arcadia. He weaves a brilliantly pagan eroticism, at once tender, yet forceful and hard, like the hard-shelled seeds that spring from the fragilest of flowers. These poems are both, and in that breadth, nothing short of extraordinary."—Trebor Healey, author of *Sweet Son of Pan* and *Through It Came Bright Colors*

"Jeff Mann is the Sappho of Appalachia. I can think of no higher or truer praise. Like the legendary Lesbian bard, Mann roots the exquisite, fragmentary psalms and prayers that make up *On the Tongue* with extremely specific details and locales that become, word by word and beat by beat, universal and unforgettable flowerings, and all because of these two poets' deceptively simple art of singing hauntingly of that forever universal theme: desire, as deferred and sated by both gods and mortals."—Ian Philips, author of *Satyriasis* and *See Dick Deconstruct*

"Jeff Mann combines a deep understanding of the technical aspects of poetry with an equally profound emotional experience of loving and desiring other men. This is poetry about man-to-man sex that really works as poetry. This volume is simultaneously arousing, tragic, nostalgic, and serene. Mann's work is solidly grounded in the legends and landscapes of the South. Reading these poems, you stand beside him on a mountainside given over to autumn colors; you savor a rough kiss with the welcome scrape of a beard; and you remember every love that slipped through your fingers. Mann is one of those few writers who uses language as carefully as a painter dips into his palette."—Patrick Califia, author of *Mortal Companion*

"In these poems, strongly rooted in both the natural landscape and the territory of the body, Jeff Mann enacts a kind of alchemy. Deeply conscious of our temporal condition, the poet more fully inhabits the physical moment, melding and fusing seemingly disparate elements into something generative and new, a state in which tulips "surge open in [the] throat" and the lover's heart is "peat starred, / a pulsing mud." Passionate, assertive, tender, masculine, and wholly attentive to our place in and of this world, here are poems of a kindred spirit whose voice I continue to admire."—Ron Mohring, author of *Survivable World*

Other Works by Jeff Mann

Bliss

Mountain Fireflies

Flint Shards from Sussex

Bones Washed with Wine

Edge

"Devoured" in *Masters of Midnight: Erotic Tales of the Vampire*

Loving Mountains, Loving Men

A History of Barbed Wire

For John Ross and Cynthia Burack

Que tu viennes du ciel ou de l'enfer, qu'importe,
O Beauté! monstre énorme, effrayant, ingénu!
Si ton œil, ton souris, ton pied, m'ouvrent la porte
D'un Infini que j'aime et n'ai jamais connu?

—"Hymne à la Beauté," Charles Baudelaire

Contents

The Mourning Dove

Blessing on the Tongue

The Mourning Dove

Doom

You have grown a beard
since I saw you last, since
I swore you off. Dark,

with a little silver
around the chin.
I drop my suitcase,

I open my arms,
my strength at an end.
You grin and ascend

the last steps between us.
For the doomed,
dignity's the final prayer.

Now flood waters lap
over the levee. The meteor
embeds itself in earth.

Prisms

Of course I brought champagne,
nipple clamps, cock rings and condoms.
Those who must part in only hours
compose their touch, their time,

in the most intense colors they can find.
Pollen dust in charcoal beards.
Bruises' plum. Red rope-chafe,
the melt of pearls.

A prism hangs in the window
of your marriage, breaking light
across your face. These refrac-
tions, all I get to keep.

Warmth

In your absence, what's left of the world?
Timetables, itineraries of wind.

The search for warmth,
consolation, beautiful distraction.

Some substitute for your body.
Candles lit before

St. Sebastian in Salzburg.
In Dublin, St. Valentine's bones.

In Thessaloniki, a chapel Christ with bound hands.
Banks of votive candles I held

cold palms above, the sun-warm poppy-
strewn stones of the Acropolis,

Swiss glühwein cupped and sipped
in the bitter breath of Roseg glacier.

In Brussels, furtively stroking the black marble
nipples of straining Prometheus,

the finely carved armpit hair.
In Bern, the white marble chest of Christ

collapsed into pietà. Palmfuls
of seawater chilly at St. Andrews,

Santorini, Chalkidiki.
Three years. Now my hands come back to you.

Pines

Far above the earth
the needled boughs are brushing,
intermingling. Moist and black
after rain, edged with silver,
the mats of hair between our hearts.

What is sacred?
Not beauty but the tenderness
it evokes. So a lover finally returns
to what he finds most beautiful,
another man sighing beneath him,
high wind soughing through
a pine too old to name.

Arrival

How long this starlight has yearned
for the earth. It falls across

my forehead now, your bare shoulders.
Everything is silence

save the small sound of your sleep.

Mercy

and the gratitude
in its wake—

clean water my ancestors gulped
after afternoons haying,

welling between the splayed roots of oak.
And on the night of the full moon,

this alchemy: the pussywillow blooms,

pollen a powdering of gold dust,
flame ground to meal.

You whisper my name
as I move inside you.

Tulips surge open in my throat.

Return

Long years apart.
Now I pull off your jeans,

then mine. I fall to my knees,
fill my mouth, bury my face in fur.

So the golden warbler roosts at last.
Even in sleep its tiny claws curl about the twig.

So, after years of Sahara, years of war,
my father, all Antaeus, took up

a clump of West Virginia earth.
He must have wept.

He must have wept like this.
Handfuls—

not of sand.
Of soil. Of soil.

Indelible

Resin hisses from the ends
of green pine kindling tossed
on the fire. With a sticky finger,
with semen's liquid moonstone,

I scrawl your initials on my brow.
What allows the indelible?
Not the pen but the strength
of the medium marked.

Thaw

Along the sycamore-haunted
streams of West Virginia,

the last ice edging rocks
breaks loose, dissolves.

I cinch the ropes across your chest.
Naked, you lean against me,

shaking and sighing,
entirely vulnerable.

Frost is melting
on the bedroom windowpane,

sweat trickles down your sides.
The only agony prayed for, that of thaw.

Steel

From these fervid arms
so many lovers have shied.

Wood recognizing its weakness.
The well-advised cowardice

of ditchweeds
brittle with autumn.

Long after the wildfire embrace,
interstices of char.

Beneath the surface,
the bones of burnt roots burn on.

You,
if only for brief intervals,

you step inside the flame.
In the oak-coals,

you hammer out the steel.
Sharper, stronger.

Along your sword's edge
the fire laps and sparks.

Sap-Rise

For the first time inside me,
you buck up against ropes

binding you to the bed.
I straddle your waist,

stroke your dark chest hair,
clench you hard.

Antlers honed against bark,
your growls merge with mine.

Asleep so long, do the maples
ache in spring, in early sap-rise?

At the spile-tip, sun seizes
sugar-water's first drop.

The dark taproot
thrusts deeper into earth.

Ice

I wake first,
to a mourning dove's triple sobbing.
You sleep on, back to me.

Sometimes even touch
is superfluous. The blue shadow
of spruce retreats,

the gray fangs of frost dissolve.
This ice has enameled
my body for years.

It splinters off
this morning, peacefully,
bits of laboratory glass, cicada husk.

As if a dogwood wedge
were set over my breastbone,
the oak maul brought down,

a cracking along the corewood.
The smallness of your shoulders
shards my heart.

Salt

My tears or your sweat?
Burning my eyes
the way kirsch melts
the mouth. Any sweet
distills into scorch.

Extremes well up our origins,
our wilderness, salt deposits
towards which animals
track their forest trails.
We evaporate like seawater.

What mingled minerals
we leave behind: a warmth
abruptly ended, a chalk
outline on asphalt.

Prometheus

Prometheus,
you have set a torch to my bones.
The marrow smokes and smoulders,
a mine fire no one can stop.

This is your punishment—
exposed, roped to this rock.
Tiny pterodactyl beaks
twist hungrily at each nipple bud.

When another's lips brush your chest,
wince. My name will break
from your body like the coiling
green of tulip leaves, these early

ascensions from late, from last snow.

In Ireland

Lapsed Catholic,
you should understand.
In Ireland, the straining chest
of every savior reminded me of you.

They burn the body of the earth
in Longford, Sligo, Kerry.
The slow hearth-smoulder, every square inch
of your grassy muscles moving over mine.

The scent of peat, your armpits
after biking long. I wiped
Guinness foam from my moustache,
pub after pub. Church after church,

Christ's heart was bared, bleeding,
wrapped in thorns. I pounded
my breastbone,
I lit a votive candle.

In the shadows, someone
always knelt, as if on the cliff-
edge where Ireland ends in sea.

Pelt

I had forgotten
in those longs years apart—
how dark with hair

your belly, chest and back.
The rich pelt of remnant bears,

laurel hells on Salt Pond Mountain,
emerald shade beneath the last

virgin hemlock stand,
two men entering
the wilderness together.

Gray

Gray in your beard—
trickles along the chin

as if you were chewing silver.
Snow lies along the oak branches

like moonlight crystallized.
In the boughs of black spruce

this flock of pewter birds ruckuses
with dusk, then comes to rest.

All night wind soughs and smoothes
their mile-rough feathers, the miracle

long migrations make of home.

Holiness

Gregorian chants,
a stick of frankincense.

Your T-shirt peeled off
like black bud scales.

Your nipples, a crocus defiance
I take between my teeth.

My face in your armpits—
a stag at a salt lick,

the scent of carpet mosses,
the first March thaw.

Heartbeat

My hands cup your forehead,
cup your hairy breast, your pulse

slowed with sleep, as if
I could press my palm against

a grassy hillside,
hold my breath, and

feel the heartbeat of the earth.

Piedmont

Gifts come after
that first frenzy subsides,
so many settled lovers swore.
Piedmont I never glimpsed before.

On the futon-couch we cram popcorn,
sip Pilsner Urquell, watch TV.
You drowse off, too much to drink,
head in my lap. This is bliss:

for hours, calm,
I watch you sleep, stroking
runes along your brow, through
your graying, thinning hair.

Grace

What is grace but

your fingers tracing my face,
my brow's braille,

your beard brushing
my near-bare scalp.

Crucifixion

Over the entrance
        to Sligo Cathedral,
                Christ is crucified.
                        Glazed with sudden sun,

his muscles arch,
        the pained strain
                of marble, his head
                        bows in submission.

Bearded savior,
        in twilight's indigo
                you are stripped, silenced,
                        bound spread-eagle to the bed.

Inside the shrine, I light
        two candles. Their wax
                turns translucent, pools
                        together, makes new forms.

Devouring

I release the rubber beaks.
Agony's a blood-rush,

screams stifled
by your own jockstrap.

My hand clamps
your jaw, my lips gentling,

nuzzling nipples
till your bucking

moans subside.
Sweet whimpers,

mouthfuls of Lindisfarne mead
I sip from a silver quaich.

This is the devouring we've waited for.
Tonight let me bring you to tears,

leave a mark that will not fade,
a touch become a tattoo.

Fingerprints

Reach in here
beneath the breastbone.
My heart's peat-starred,
a pulsing mud.

Press your fingertips in hard,
leave impressions the way
gingko and fern once did
in natal shale. I will be

your record, once a long
burning, a great weight,
make dense an organ so soft.
The metamorphosis

begins with the pressure
of your body on mine.
Already my heart is charring to coal.
Soon your fingerprints will be diamond.

Mines

Sleep apart if you will.
With some distance between us—

the cold gap of sheets that so used to hurt—
I can study your beauty better.

Keep your mystery.
I have given up pickax and shovel.

It is enough to nuzzle the apple blooms,
the early needles of the larch,

to stain my fingers with resin, to catch
on my tongue drops of sweet sap trickling

from maple wounds the woodpeckers left.
What coal seams, what gold ores, reserve or reveal

as you will. I want nothing
but to stretch naked across these hillocks,

between my fingers and teeth
gently stroke the pasture grass.

Magnolia

One arm
beneath your shoulders,
one beneath your knees,

I lift you bound into my arms.
Helplessness dark
as wildflower honey,

some sacrament sticky
between our lips.
The trust

of pollen's elisions
along the wind,
the saucer magnolia

opening all those
pink mouths to gulp
late winter sun,

despite fatalism,
the likely risks,
late frost.

Peace

Late February, late morning
sunlight pours over the bed

benedictions, clover honey
on a communion wafer.

You sprawl on your belly now,
beard buried in the pillow.

I am too happy to sleep.

Across your back, currents of hair,
the long wave of water weeds

where peat-dark river rushes
into Sligo Bay. Is this peace?

To study the world and know
I would change nothing.

Topographies

It is the curse of perspective:
ridgetop and bottomland,
how each defines the other.

Hillocks of your chest. Between them,
thick fir-forest, soft darkness where,
given choice, I would rest my face forever.

How love's described
topographically: great
as a mountain, deep
as a canyon.

Beneath my tongue the sandstone strains.
Hard shoulders and arms restrained,
hands bound behind your back.
Your legs lock around my waist, I slide inside,
I lift you into my arms.

How even the memory
of superlatives makes petty
every other pleasure.

Soon enough, morning fog obscuring maple limbs.
Keyboard beneath my fingertips.
Mountains run out, paper's flat plane.
Moustache hair in my mouth. Not yours. My own.

Earth-Fire

Beneath the thin tissues of soil,
beneath the bones of bedrock,
the marrow of the earth is fire.

See how it escapes to flicker
in the sunlight, to meet
heat with heat? In the pale emerald

of iris blades ascending,
in the graveyard's new grasses,
the smoky hair across our jaws,

our bellies and groins and chests.

Clutch

The teleology of thumbs
and fingerbones, to clutch.

Tomorrow, sycamore bark
must flake off. The skin

is soon sloughed,
frail cells
through which we touch.

Wind is the tourniquet between us,
stopping the blood flow from twig to leaf.

So many leaves are "palmate,"
we call it: shaped like hands.

Gold to jade, embers to ash.
Tomorrow, only the steering wheel

beneath my palms. Bound to leave bruises,
any grasp condemned to end so soon.

Alba

Alba is the color of separation,
the white of aging hair, of bone,

the mourning dove's lost feathers,
dawn's first seep, dawn

of the day lovers allot to part.
Alba, the pale skin revealed when

rings are removed, when fractured water breaks
on rocks. White, the light reflected, not kept.

Dove

The mourning dove's lament sees winter out,
triptych in which meeting, loving, parting
are folded into one. I heard its dirge

when we first shook hands, each rare
morning we woke together, the day you left,
and all the years apart. Now I stroke

gray strands about your temples, about
your chin, I prepare to part with grace.
Now the mourning dove with a shudder

lands on the balcony rail. It tips about,
balances along the breeze, peers at us,
then vanishes in a whir of wings.

Rusts

This rusts our touch—
the tiny chisels of acid rain
pitting the Parthenon, centuries
of candle smoke smudging the chapel ceiling,
weather's sandpapers blurring
the etched names on graves.

In Falls Church, Virginia,
a weekend ends. Your head
adrowse in my lap, you smile up
at me once and close your eyes.
I cock my wrist to check the time.

The shadow slips past the breakfast nook.
In sun's tilted lance, motes
of dust too sluggish to dance.

Along Roosevelt Avenue, the shush
of traffic never ceases.

Volatiles

Now the elevator door cancels out your smile,
the dove mourns in pines above the parking lot.
Indigo evening, I turn into traffic headed south.

Brief remnants of a blessing,
these bruises aching along my thigh,
your musk still scenting my fingertips.

For light, we pay willingly whatever price is asked—
sorrow deep as the love for what's lost.
Behind my brow, our firepit's embers dwindle,

winter reasserts itself, your muscle and bone
dissolve. How rapidly love moves
from memory to solid, then back again.

The bottle of moonshine's uncapped.
All that is volatile abandons the body,
all that is flammable escapes into air.

Blessing on the Tongue

Late May Mountain Gifts

First peas, tiny rumbles in a zinc bowl.
Fresh strawberries over buttermilk biscuits.
Earliest lettuce-bibs, wilted Appalachian
under hot vinegar and bacon grease,
sharper with new scallions. And this year,

this May, amidst more predictable petals,
a demon lover named for a saint.
Drunk on strawberry coladas, grabbing indiscreet
pec handfuls, insulting my taste in music,
you are keeping tension taut between us,
the precarious stretch of dulcimer strings.
You earn your punishment. In spasms

the leaves are luminous, the honeysuckle
air ignites, clouds dart with tiny lightnings,
like skin shivering under the softest
brush of moustache or breath. Limbs bound,
speech and sight sealed, you give your body whole.
How not then a bit of soul, as this spring surpasses
all springs, all gifts, in your giving.

Lover, humanity floods back with hunger.
I am taught again how to treasure,
as I click the cuffs into place, lick a trickle
of late-May heat from your temple, from
the shaking hair above your heart.

Downs

This Sunday, hard Sussex rain on the panes
wakes me early. Nothing to curl warmly against

save bunched comforter, memory.
Rising for tea, taking up the pen,

the pen; to one almost always elsewhere,
speaking on white sheets of slaughtered trees.

This is one brand of life, the dole
Marcus Aurelius says we must accept

to be happy. I admit it at last:
I will never be happy, if happy

is thanking God for what feels always
like alms. The South Downs

have more sense, less ambition.
Brandishing their hedgerows,

their Scotch broom, they swell
towards the sea, the plumpness

of the well-fed, beer-enthused thirties
I chastise in my mirror every morning.

Even you take Lean Cuisine
to work with you now, complaining of

your gut, your gray hairs, the glasses
you will be wearing when next we meet.

Beauty aging is easier to love.
It is less terrible, more human.

Those rare mornings together, I woke
before you, trying to memorize

your full cheeks, beard-stubble like
scatters of volcanic sand,

grading white about the chin.
Flesh gathers beneath your jaw,

talus heaps at the chalk-cliff's foot.
Downs I would smooth beneath me

until they end sheer in sea—your chest,
your belly, topoi of shoulders and buttocks,

the grass-thick swells that drop like bone
into matching swells of foam.

Nettles

Per ardua ad astra,
the headstone claims,

as if pain were a subway card,
a ticket punched for

some destination—yes, destiny's
embedded in it—

better than any
we could have chosen

ourselves. To find at last
the body's purpose

and then to lose it?
At last after all

these years I have driven you
to tears. Swapping seas.

Pressing scar to scar
till they bloom again

and the liquors mix.
In my beard, your brine

blended with mine,
the mingling at Gibraltar.

At every ocean's edge I bend,
dip a finger, taste.

Today, about neglected graves,
the nettles frowse.

This hand with which I scrawled
my name in liquid opal on your back,

this hand with which I wiped dry
your cheek—I thrust my fingers in.

Minor needles.
Poison's intoxicant,

pain's a lens,
bending the dark

rays to a point.
The romantic in me

stroking nettles.
Never to be numb again.

Roosevelt Island

All I keep of that afternoon
is how you joked amidst the woods

about "the garden path." How I
looked both ways, furtive as a thief,

before I kissed you briefly
surrounded by pawpaws and patches

of a wildflower I could not name.
How you had not shaved for days

to please me, so love would be
abrasive, would leave stubble-burn.

How I plucked a sprig
of bedstraw and tossed it against

your shirt where with tiny claws
it clung. How you hesitated

for a second or two before
you plucked it off and let it fall.

Greek Groans

Testing my tiny comprehension
of Greek as I rode the buses
through Thessaloniki, I strained
to read the street signs before
they'd flashed past. Aristotelous,
Egnatia. "The triangle is soft
th or *d*, *L* the upside-down *V*,"
my guidebook would gasp.

Your conversations were as opaque,
your hand casually gripping mine.
All that intellect wasted on defense,
on artifice. I tried to read the language
behind the letters, like tugging
back leafy limbs before a view,
brushing dust from an archive,
an archaeological find.

Searching for some heart, some subtext
beneath the comet-glare of mind,

my body atop yours in the posture
of the Greeks, the sweat building
between my belly and your back,

your groans difficult
to decipher as delta, lambda, rho,

wondering if my teeth on your nape,
my arms about your chest, my heart-
beat grafting onto yours, meant

anything at all
save exercise, wondering if any part
of me ever entered save flesh.

Would-Be Husband Turns Whore

I

There was a rawhide-thong bondage-romp
near Pipestem, relaxed on gin and weed-
with-roots-in-hell, the cabin loft a coziness
beneath the mirrored, rain-sounding ceiling.

Then a three-way after much pasta, much
aphrodisiac neon rosé, taking turns with
the harness and cuffs, alternating participant
and spectator in a Blacksburg blue movie.

Next a seminar in Morgantown—
the obligatory "Sir," poseurs
of biceps and pecs, paddling a stranger
under the moon, a fine view of
Star City and the stadium
from the asphalt heights of Law Center Hill.

Finally California: meticulously safe
in the Castro, playing with clamps
and ball gag and Absolut buzz.
Then that gully on Mount Diablo, the restraint
one gray bandana can provide, smell of sagebrush,
litter of live oak leaves, and the aftermath
of bruised nipples and weeds in my underwear.

Tonight, in all likelihood, the list continues.
Lover, I am grieving differently now.
Hot to be your husband, sick of sainthood,
this year in your wake I opt to be a whore.

2

Crown vetch clambers, purpling July
and feathery, over the roadcuts now,
over anticlines of colored coals,
shales, limestones, sandstones.
Beneath the heaping compost of time,
the heat has fused and flattened the sea's
silicas, the delicate swamp mosses,
the sweep of fern, the stubborn bump
of bone, skull, and spiralled shell.

Frantic palimpsest, promiscuity.
Body after body after body, the act
always more arousing than the man.
Beneath the garnered sweat and
sediment of strangers, I try

to bury your body, luminous still
even in absence. When will
the paint of the present prove
at last opaque, the fire
snuff out beneath the shoveled soil,
the breath beneath the pillow cease?

The Soundtrack to *Sophie's Choice*

(for Cindy Burack)

Someone else must live there now—
3446 Connecticut Avenue #402—
that borrowed apartment where he and I last
made love. Smells of cooking still linger
in the hallways, sirens shriek along
the avenue, car stereos thump at the red light.
That room where I unfolded the futon, confident
after so many years that we would continue—
that space is clogged now with couch or television,
rent-control grandmothers or mewling brats.

July heat. I put the *Sophie's Choice* soundtrack
on repeat, poured mead in matching pewter quaichs
I'd just bought us in Edinburgh. Mead, then
Atholl Brose, chrism on his brow, his lips,
spilled deliberately into his thick chest hair's
storm cloud, the slow sticky savor of lapping up.

I love you, he sighed afterwards, in answer to
nothing. *You're a wonderful lover. So good
to me*. I lay amazed, afraid to believe,
the fiery cross of his shoulder tattoo
between my lips like bread. Then, unlike
Nathan and Sophie—no final freeze,
then fade, vignettes permitting perfection—
we rose from sheets that had shrouded
our ascension (*together* is always a guess).
He carefully showered off the scent of me,
his nipples sticky with mead, still raw

with my teeth's reverence. At the door—
had he decided already this time was the last?—
Thomas demanded one more hug. I walked him
to the Metro—always the hurry to beat
his lover home—I tried to catch one final
glimpse of his face in the train window rushing
by but missed it. Back in Cindy's apartment,
I lay down in lavender twilight, listened
to the music, finished the mead.

What we miss, perhaps, is not the ones
we adored, but illusions they allowed.
How I used to swagger the streets, whistling,
whispering his name, tossing up and catching
my keys, stars pulsing in my solar plexus,
believing at last I was loved in return.

The Ladies Mile Pub

How redeemable, how golden
the world seems, through the bottom
of a pint of Scrumpy Jack cider.

A white streak like sycamore bark,
like lightning strike, snakes along
the bartender's forearm.

What the damaged dream of:
someone to say
All your scars are beautiful.

Coconut Fried Pie

Worn denim, redneck
cap, scuffed boots and beard—

I'm just another gruff mountain man
biting into a coconut fried pie

in street-fair sunlight by the Baptist church.
The crust is a mock resistance;

the man, tied belly-down,
groans once, gives way.

From his dark moss-cleft
I nuzzle cream of coconut.

The four-poster shakes,
he bites the sheets,

bucks back
against my tongue, against my beard.

Fantasia in the English Garden

Above beer garden tables, black locust drips
down the scent of butterscotch. After hours
of touring Munich—the Residenz, the Frauenkirche—
I heft myself into this seat to rest sore legs,
sore feet, limping left hip. How inexhaustibly
I used to walk. Service at the Seehaus is slow
but sexy. The waiter's body is half my age,
muscled, compact. When he bends towards me
with a glass of yeast-clouded wheat beer,
I want to reach up, stroke his dark goatee.

Down by the lake edge, in the sun's heat
the young are crowding, loud and cheerful.
Lean waists, brown arms, the erratic gestures
of the inebriated. Watching them, thirstily
I suck down my beer, savor the scent of cloves.
Something widens between us, the glittering
satin of summer, unruffled as their skin.
In meadows across the lake, the nudist
section every tourist's curiosity wings around,
all the skin is old, fabrics without water's forgetfulness,
wrinkled with the history of every storm endured.

Beach of sagging seals. How does one learn
to love what is less than beautiful? What is bitter?
What is haunted? When the goateed waiter,
Tadzio, as I have christened him, heads for the bathroom,
I follow him, convinced he's given me the eye.
I lock the door behind us, turn into his surprised smile,
rip his shirt open and off. The buttons explode
like touch-me-not seeds, overripe, tiny clatters

on the tiles. In thick moss swirling up the trunks
of Alpine evergreens, in his black chest hair
I bury my face, I pinch and bite his nipples
till they bruise. Now I'm roping his wrists
behind his back, knotting a musty cloth
between his teeth, shoving his pants down
around his ankles, bending him over the sink,
gripping his waist, his sex, pushing into him.

We scatter ourselves like black locust pollen.
Still gasping, hearts slowing, I dip my forefinger
into molten quartz he's spattered on the faucet,
I lift droplets like blood or maple sap to my lips.
As I taste, the silver in my beard begins to darken.

Ghost and Vampire Tour, New Orleans

At dusk we congregate
about Lafitte's Blacksmith Shop,
those for whom reality's insufficient,
daylight's dull. The guide jokingly
passes out some garlic, a wooden stake,
leads us by lamplight all about the Quarter.
Here's Madame Lalaurie's, where the cries
of chained slaves still startle
the living. The Sultan's retreat,
site of a mysterious massacre.
Miriam's Voodoo Temple, with her
sleepy snake, icons of Urzuli
and Baron Samedi, offerings of rum.
Marie Laveau's old home, where
an eldritch fire claimed a recent owner.
And this alleyway, where the bodies
of two men were found hanging,
drained of blood. The Anne Rice fans
lap at this: what we came for.

In a Rampart Street bar we take a break.
A few blocks up the street the dead
are baking like bread in their oven tombs.
Somewhere nearby, Christ is stripped
to the waist, nailed down in marble.
Somewhere the night jasmine
blooms, the shrivelled resurrection fern
waits for rain. I order a Hurricane-
to-go—decadence cheap and legal—deep red
with grenadine, the juice of Persephone's

pomegranate, ruby seeds the dead
break spurtingly between their teeth.
In a deep lounge chair I settle back
amidst other chatting tourists, and
I study him: khaki shorts, white T-shirt,
black vest. Wavy dark hair, Mediterranean
eyes, goatee, the hoop of his earring
glinting, glinting the black gloss of his
forearm hair. Heartbeat like a solemn
voodoo drum. I veil my stare, sip
the Hurricane, fish out the maraschino
cherry, close my eyes
and nip—

Against his thrashing,
I force him down, clamp his mouth.
His eyes are wet—onyx mirrors,
moonlight misting the bottom of a well.
Smiling, I smooth his eyebrows.
Beneath my tongue the hair
of his chest is Spanish moss,
his nipples are azalea buds,
his neck's unshaven stubble
the salty black grit of volcanic sand.
Now the taste of rust. And this welling,
welling, heartbeat
caught beneath my fangs.

"Time to go!" yells the guide above some
vulgar jukebox beat. I wipe my beard,
flip the cherry stem into the ashtray,
rise, follow my victim out. Over the gypsum-
white cemetery wall, the white moth flits,
follows the scent of night-blooming jasmine.

Finds the flower, buries its head, itself,
in the frayed white petals, sips—*blessed*,
blessed—hovers and purrs and sips.

Monster

I

Sauna stranger, clad
only in a jockstrap,
he's jogging in place

to work up a fast
sweat, using a
credit card as a strigil.

So lean—beneath his belly
hair the ripple of muscles,
parentheses inside parentheses,

the way water wells over
a submarine spring,
a school of fish ascending.

As if his skin were
a scrim, pale pearl-
fog dawn skims through.

Master of peripheral vision,
I watch his hairy chest
bounce. And when

he settles on the cedar
bench and leans forward,
elbows on his knees,

if I lean casually
back in a studied stretch,
I can see his buttock

curves dark with fur—
stones worn smooth
by an ancient river,

now softened with thick moss.
Late peaches fallen in
high orchard grass—

the juice, sun-brewed,
would glaze a beard,
would make a man drunk.

2

The purpose of perfection?
To teach us longing.
To make us monsters.

3

I have always been the monster,
waiting there, on the edges

of your eyes, where mist turns solid,
where it presses its wings against

lamplit windowpanes and flowers
into frost. Where breath makes

circles on the glass,
all night I watch you sleep.

Uninvited, I depart at dawn,
leaving no footprints in the snow.

4

Those orchards of my childhood,
above the cliffs on Tunnel Hill—
how wildly the yellow

jackets circled about
late fallen peaches.
How deeply they burrowed

into flesh and drowned.
I have been dead
a long time.

How wildly
those imperfect dream
of possessing perfection

in another.
Every glimpse
of beauty's

a mouthful
of blood,
of heartbeat.

My own sauna-sweat's
a tarnished silver,
the scent of cumin

and cedar trees,
an Inverness cape
I wrap about me.

My bone marrow's
frost, the earth's
overripe. One puncture,

two,
and the lava,
released,

wells
between my lips.
You dull ones,

always in the middle,
striders along noon,
what do you know of

the edges,
the ecstasies of
dawn and dusk,

the pulse of
perfection filling
your mouths, slowing,

slowing. A rill of sweat
trails down a stranger's spine,
disappears like a silver

tongue,
like a beckoning,
along the mossy cleft.

I am alive
only when
my fangs ache.

Sated sleepers,
only the famished
are awake.

Porno Poem

On command the bottom strips and sits,
eyes lowered. With cotton rope the Top
ties his wrists behind him, ties his ankles
to the chair legs, then—slow dervish—
wraps rope round and round his boy's
belly and chest. Next, a black blindfold.
Finally, two white socks knotted
at the toes, then forced between his teeth.

The Top sits nearby, smoking, reading
a newspaper, occasionally tugging hard
at tweezer-clamps hanging from
his slave's nipples. Sweat trickles down
the bottom's sides. He struggles, surrenders,
chews the gag and groans. Inside him,

the sea's incessant waves subside,
the asteroid stops its weary circling.
Christ forgives the spear, the thorns,
the nails, feels earth and sky meet and meld
beneath his breastbone, the sun's glare go out.

The Vampire Explains

I am helpless in the face of that scent.
Late-summer yellow jackets are drowning

themselves in windfall orchards, weaving
drunken down long naves of peach.

I am helpless in the face of that music,
the slow chest-heave of a man after labor,

the dark rise and fall of that estuary
beneath mounds of muscle, the thick hair

over the torso, pulse beating beneath
an unshaven neck, waves rippling black sand.

I am the spear in the savior's side, driven in
hard. Beneath my blade, the wound spills

over, like oozy seed-pearls of okra, oyster liqueur,
pomegranate seeds scattered across curves of snow.

Long ago the grapes were grown and harvested,
trampled, seething for years in your bodies' vats,

your daily grails. My fangs decant them.
Salt, like semen's sudden cumulus.

Sugar, like summer's long-gathered honey,
amber dripping from broken cells of wax.

And rust, the taste of steel weakening,
decay I am born to forestall. Dark butterfly,

my face burrows into the necks or breasts
of the beautiful, my lips press the sugar

maple's tapped trunk, sipping sap pumped
straight from the heart of the hills.

My beard's dewed with rubies, sticky
with syrup. This is how I love the earth.

Kilts

By midnight we have closed our door
on the rest of it—bagpipes and banquet food,
toasts and guitars—Burns Night at Hotel Roanoke.
Ours is a fine room, with a view over railroad tracks,
the downtown market, the star atop Mill Mountain,
but what's most important tonight is the width
of the bed, which we size up the way an athlete
eyes a playing field, imagining all the feints,
rushes and strategems such space allows.
We are only halfway through Scapa nightcaps
before our kilts erect their tent-poles, before
I begin to undress us both. Shoes, flashes, and
socks first, then Prince Charlie coatees, vests,
tuxedo shirts and ties, peeling off
the centuries, till, still kilted, we are two
bare-chested, barefoot men of any era,
one standing on tiptoe to kiss the other,
chest hair blending, soft larch needles,
bough brushing bough in highland storm.
I push you back onto the bed, gulp Scotch,
then kiss you—our mouths mingling malt
and Orkney peat, our kilt belts and sporrans
clicking together, tartans mixing like firths
where mountain streams meet sea.
It's a huge plaid bell of heather I fold back
and duck beneath like a tent flap, burrowing
like a bumblebee entering the tabernacle.
Here are wine and bread, the great pistil
throbbing between my lips, cathedral
bell's tongue I tongue, drops of seawater,
darkness beneath the altar cloth.

***

We were always there, among the clans—
hidden like the small dark in throats
of flowers, the shade beneath spruce
where snow lies blue and long—
rare like sprays of heather blooming
white amidst the common purple.
We drove sheep, harvested crops,
sharpened claymore and battleax,
mashed the barley in the still.
Our eyes met in church and pasture,
over the fishnets. Some of us were caught
together, dragged before the congregation,
were knifed or burnt or driven out.
Others fought and fell, raven food
like all the rest, with Wallace
at Stirling Bridge, with the Bruce
at Bannockburn, with Prince Charlie
at Culloden. On the eve of battle,
we took what comfort, what farewells
we could, meeting in tents pitched
deliberately distant, in hay lofts or glens,
sheltered hill-coves where the heather
first blooms, larch thickets where
one man knelt before another,
slipping first hands, then head beneath
his lover's kilt, while the other leaned
back against hay-bale or bedstead or
tree trunk, thrust and sighed, prayed
against intruders, discovery, hell.
Tonight we make love with you,
through you, as you finally unstrap
your clean, expensive kilts, as you roll together

across an elegant bed, sleep close and safe
all night, as you rise guiltless for showers
and breakfast buffet, the magnolia leaves
beneath your window gleaming in winter sun—
polished sword blades, battle flags whipping in wind.

Olive Oil

She struck the rock
where now Caryatids stare out
over smog. She struck the rock
and up leapt the first olive tree,

feathering silver-green in Attic
sunlight. What gift could match it?
Poseidon defeated, Athena
was pronounced patron of Athens.

You arrive at sunset with a bottle
of retsina and a mysterious bag
you put by the bed. While October
ignites its maple bonfires

about the house and the crickets
yearn and keen for any inlet
into warmth, we pour the wine,
set out the feta and herb bread,

feed one another glossy olives.
The taut-hipped calamata,
plump queen of the Peloponnesians.
The bitter, lemon-scented green.

The shrivelly oil-cured, so glitter-
black you'd think obsidian
had become a snack.
The gnawed-bare pits pile up.

In the bedroom afterwards,
you strip us both, then,
grinning, unpack your surprises:
a big bottle of olive oil,

a jade-green shower curtain
you stretch out across the bed.
A little goes a long way.
A few dribbles over hairy chest,

buttock or groin, and suddenly
we are Greco-Roman wrestlers
smeared with struggle's sweat.
Golden as icons, our muscles gleam,

the sheen sunset stretches over
the sea, dew glittering along
the webby rosaries of dawn.
We are lapping slippery skin, sliding

slick flesh through our fists till laughing
shudders, spasms, the sweet pant-hot
exhaustion, two men curled together
in the shadows of the olive grove.

One Definition of the Perfect Lover

In the kitchen, a chef.
In the bedroom, a whore.

For dinner, my lover lights candles,
pours Clos du Bois, lays out

roasted red pepper hummus,
penne heaped with shrimp.

For dessert—
and isn't the juxtaposition

of event often as delicious
as events themselves?—

he ties my hands
to the headboard of the bed,

nuzzles my nipples raw,
force-feeds me Sambuca

on the tip of his cock.

Triptypch

i. The Fitzwilliam Museum, Cambridge

A bas-relief from Persepolis,
from the Palace of Xerxes.
The marker reads: "Two bearded

and long-haired courtiers shown
in a comradely gesture."
Their muscles are stylized,

stone curves I want to run
my fingers along. One man
rests his hand on the other's

shoulder, the second strokes
his companion's beard. From his belt,
a sword hangs between them,

angling up, its blade shaped
like a penis. It thrusts
through all the centuries

separating once-warm skin
from sunlight today,
from the way

I suddenly turn to stroke
your temples, gray
ripples amidst the gold.

2. Trinity College, Cambridge

In the elegant New Guest Room,
its windows rich with wisteria bloom,
after taking tea, devouring

fried bread, eggs, bacon, bangers,
two men are taking a bath,
two big bodies wedged together

in that tiny tub, soaping belly hair
into a lather and laughing.
From travel-sore soles, the ache

is massaged: long walks about the Tower,
St. Paul's, Soho and Trafalgar Square.
The reverence of Primitive Baptists,

washing one another's feet, as if
all of us could be saviors, if only of
ourselves. Then the maid's voice

suddenly shards the peace,
slipping in with her key to clear out
the breakfast leavings. Through the half-

open bathroom door, her cheery
greeting, the clatter of teapot and flatware
only yards away. The lovers leap

from the bath, dry off and dress
hurriedly, wondering what year it is
here, worrying where the laws stand.

3. Père Lachaise

In a poor hotel on the Left Bank
Oscar Wilde supposedly said,
"Either that wallpaper goes or

I do," just before he died,
only two years beyond the ruin
of Reading Gaol, forced labor

where large rocks
were hammered into small.
Amidst emerald smoke,

the horse chestnuts
of Père Lachaise,
his tomb's a naked angel

in flight, spreading
huge Assyrian wings.
The victim of modern Vandals:

its muscles marred
with graffiti tattoos,
its penis broken off.

John's Apple Pie

Heroically I have resisted
a comfortable happiness, decades
snuffling after handsome liars,
the already-married, the ones
who live for listeners and mirrors,
those who talk too much, as if the sound
of their voices was all they needed
to give and the world ought to be damned
grateful for that. Forgive me, then,

for my present confusion.
When I stroke the dark waves
that roll across your chest and break
about your throat, when my eyes meet
yours the way water deepens sapphire
beneath the capes and jetties of Greece,
when I tongue-comb your body's garden
and harvest cumin-smoke, peach-cleft,
the clear sticky sap of okra, its spill
of tiny pure-white pearls,

some part of me is calm.
I do not want to bite down till
your breast breaks and my teeth run
red with pomegranate juice. Bridge-edges
no longer tempt me, or long walks
in thunderstorms or cemeteries, or
those worm-casing mountain roads
where speeding straight would save
the gravediggers half a job.

This Sunday I have apples
to peel, Granny Smith, a bowlful,
while you roll out piecrust.
Your grandmother's recipe,
your grandmother's rolling pin
and pastry sock. While the pie bakes,
some Stilton, some wine, then
rosemary pork chops, potatoes,
half-runners cooked Southern-style
with bacon grease. Finally, apple pie
with ice cream—that complex mingle
of sweet, creamy, tart. For a few minutes,
here and there, it's all exactly as we want it—
peace and passion in perfect balance,
balance like blessing on the tongue.

Books Available from Gival Press

A Change of Heart by David Garrett Izzo

1st edition, ISBN 1-928589-18-9, (ISBN 13: 978-1-928589-18-1), $20.00

A historical novel about Aldous Huxley and his circle "astonishingly alive and accurate."
— Roger Lathbury, George Mason University

An Interdisciplinary Introduction to Women's Studies Edited by Brianne Friel & Robert L. Giron

1st edition, ISBN 1-928589-29-4, (ISBN 13: 978-1-928589-29-7), $25.00

Winner of the 2005 DIY Book Festival Award for Compilations/ Anthologies.
A succinct collection of articles written for the college student of women's studies, covering a variety of disciplines from politics to philosophy.

Bones Washed With Wine: Flint Shards from Sussex and Bliss by Jeff Mann

1st edition, ISBN 1-928589-14-6, (ISBN 13: 978-1-928589-14-3), $15.00

A special collection of lyric intensity, including the 1999 Gival Press Poetry Award winning collection. Jeff Mann is "a poet to treasure both for the wealth of his language and the generosity of his spirit."— Edward Falco, author of *Acid*

Boys, Lost & Found: Stories by Charles Casillo

1st edition, ISBN 1-928589-33-2, (ISBN 13: 978-1-928589-33-4), $20.00

Casillo's boys are hustlers, writers, models, cruisers, lovers—complicated, smart, cool, witty, lusty, and romantic. "...fascinating, often funny... a safari through the perils and joys of gay life." —Edward Field

Canciones para sola cuerda / Songs for a Single String by Jesús Gardea; English translation by Robert L. Giron

1st edition, ISBN 1-928589-09-X, (ISBN 13: 978-1-928589-09-9), $15.00

Finalist for the 2003 Violet Crown Book Award for Literary Prose & Poetry.

A moving collection of love poems, with echoes of Neruda *à la Mexicana* as Gardea writes about the primeval quest for the perfect woman. "The free verse...evokes the quality and forms of *cante hondo*, emphasizing the emotional interplay of human voice and guitar."— Elizabeth Huergo, Montgomery College

Dead Time / Tiempo muerto by Carlos Rubio

1st edition, ISBN 1-928589-17-0, (ISBN 13: 978-1-928589-17-4), $21.00

Winner of the 2003 Silver Award for Translation—ForeWord Magazine's Book of the Year.
This bilingual (English/Spanish) novel is "an unusual tale of love, hate, passion and revenge." — Karen Sealy, author of *The Eighth House*

Dervish by Gerard Wozek

1st edition, ISBN 1-928589-11-1, (ISBN 13: 978-1-928589-11-2), $15.00

Winner of the 2000 Gival Press Poetry Award.
This rich whirl of the dervish traverses a grand expanse from bars to crazy dreams to fruition of desire. "By Jove, these poems shimmer."— Gerry Gomez Pearlberg, author of *Mr. Bluebird*

Dreams and Other Ailments / Sueños y otros achaques by Teresa Bevin

1st edition, ISBN 1-928589-13-8, (ISBN 13: 978-1-928589-13-6), $21.00

Winner of the 2001 Bronze Award for Translation—ForeWord Magazine's Book of the Year.
A wonderful array of short stories about the fantasy of life and tragedy but filled with humor and hope. "*Dreams and Other Ailments* will lift your spirits."— Lynne Greeley, The University of Vermont

The Gay Herman Melville Reader Edited by Ken Schellenberg

1st edition, ISBN 1-928589-19-7, (ISBN 13: 978-1-928589-19-8), $16.00

A superb selection of Melville's work. "Here in one anthology are the selections from which a serious argument can be made by both readers and scholars that a subtext exists that can be seen as homoerotic."— David Garrett Izzo, author of *Christopher Isherwood: His Era, His Gang, and the Legacy of the Truly Strong Man*

The Great Canopy by Paula Goldman

1st edition, ISBN 1-928589-31-6, (ISBN 13: 978-1-928589-31-0), $15.00

Winner of the 2004 Gival Press Poetry Award & Semi-Finalist for the 2006 Independent Publisher Book Award for Poetry.
"Under this canopy we experience the physicality of the body through Goldman's wonderfully muscular verse as well the analytics of a mind that tackles the meaning of Orpheus or the notion of desire."—Richard Jackson, author of *Half Lives*, *Heartwall*, and *Unauthorized Autobiography: New & Selected Poems*

The Last Day of Paradise by Kiki Denis

1st edition, ISBN 1-928589-32-4 (ISBN 13: 978-1-928589-32-7), $20.00

Winner of the 2005 Gival Press Novel Award.
"...Denis's debut is a slippery in-your-face accelerated rush of sex, hokum, and Greek family life. A little bit Eurydice, a little bit Chick-lit, with non-stop riffing on reality...."—Richard Peabody, editor of *Mondo Barbie*

Let Orpheus Take Your Hand by George Klawitter

1st edition, ISBN 1-928589-16-2, (ISBN 13: 978-1-928589-16-7), $15.00

Winner of the 2001 Gival Press Poetry Award.
A thought provoking work that mixes the spiritual with stealthy desire, with Orpheus leading us out of the pit. "These poems present deliciously sly metaphors of the erotic life that keep one reading on, and chuckling with pleasure."— Edward Field, author of *Stand Up, Friend, With Me*

Literatures of the African Diaspora by Yemi D. Ogunyemi

1st edition, ISBN 1-928589-22-7, (ISBN 13: 978-1-928589-22-8), $20.00

An important study of the influences in literatures of the world. "It, indeed, proves that African literatures are, without mincing words, a fountainhead of literary divergence."—Joshua 'Kunle Awosan, University of Massachusetts Dartmouth

Maximus in Catland by David Garrett Izzo

1st edition, ISBN 1-928589-34-0, (ISBN 13: 978-1-928589-34-1), $20.00

"... [an] examination of the idea of the Truly Strong Man—or, in this case, Cat—which is one who would give his own life for the sake of transpersonal good...This book is a treat—with a truly mystical message.—Toby Johnson, author of *Secret Matter*, winner of the Lambda Literary Award for Sci-Fi

Metamorphosis of the Serpent God by Robert L. Giron

1st edition, ISBN 1-928589-07-3, (ISBN 13: 978-1-928589-07-5), $12.00

"Robert Giron's biographical poetry embraces the past and the present, ethnic and sexual identity, themes both mythical and personal."— *The Midwest Book Review*

Middlebrow Annoyances: American Drama in the 21st Century by Myles Weber

1st edition, ISBN 1-928589-20-0, (ISBN 13: 978-1-928589-20-4), $20.00

"Weber's intelligence and integrity are unsurpassed by anyone writing about the American theatre today..."— John W. Crowley, The University of Alabama at Tuscaloosa

The Nature Sonnets by Jill Williams

1st edition, ISBN 1-928589-10-3, (ISBN 13: 978-1-928589-10-5), $8.95

An innovative collection of sonnets that speaks to the cycle of nature and life, crafted with wit and clarity. "Refreshing and pleasing."— Miles David Moore, author of *The Bears of Paris*

Poetic Voices Without Borders Edited by Robert L. Giron

1st edition, ISBN 1-928589-30-8, (ISBN 13: 978-1-928589-30-3), $20.00

Winner of the 2006 Writers Notes Book Award—Notable for Art & Semi-Finalist for the 2006 Independent Publisher Book Award for Anthologies.

"...This book is edgy with a literary inclusiveness...Each voice is unique, yet together they create oneness even as they individually represent societal diversity."—Lucinda Farrokh, LareDOS: A Journal of the Borderlands

On the Altar of Greece by Donna J. Gelagotis Lee

1st edition, ISBN 1-928589-36-7, (ISBN 13: 978-1-928589-35-5), $15.00

Winner of the 2005 Gival Press Poetry Award.
"...the journey of our time at this altar offers us a striking, immense set of views of a world we thought we knew, and still, wonderfully, do know in much richer ways by the end."—Don Berger, author of *Quality Hill* and *The Cream-Filled Muse*

On the Tongue by Jeff Mann

1st edition, ISBN 1-928589-35-9, (ISBN 13: 978-1-928589-35-8), $15.00

"...brilliantly pagan eroticism, at once tender, yet forceful and hard, like the hard-shelled seeds that spring from the fragilest of flowers. These poems are both, and in that breadth, nothing short of extraordinary..."—Trebor Healey, author of *Through It Came Bright Colors*

Prosody in England and Elsewhere: A Comparative Approach by Leonardo Malcovati

1st edition, ISBN 1-928589-26-X, (ISBN 13: 978-1-928589-26-6), $20.00

"To write about the structure of poetry for a non-specialist audience takes a brave author. To do so in a way that is readable, in fact enjoyable, without sacrificing scholarly standards takes an accomplished author."—Frank Anshen, State University of New York

Secret Memories / Recuerdos secretos by Carlos Rubio

1st edition, ISBN 1-928589-27-8, (ISBN 13: 978-1-928589-27-3), $21.00

Finalist for the 2005 ForeWord Magazine's Book of Year Award for Translation.
"From the beginning, the reader feels pulled into the narrator's world and observes, along with him, a delicate, beautiful, and vulnerable universe as personal and intimate as a conversation between lovers."
—Hope Maxell Snyder, author of *Orange Wine*

The Smoke Week: Sept. 11-21, 2001 by Ellis Avery

1st edition, ISBN 1-928589-24-3, (ISBN 13: 978-1-928589-24-2), $15.00

Winner of the 2004 Writer's Notes Magazine Book Award—Notable for Culture & Winner of the Ohioana Library Walter Rumsey Marvin Award.
"Here is Witness. Here is Testimony."— Maxine Hong Kingston, author of *The Fifth Book of Peace*

Songs for the Spirit by Robert L. Giron

1st edition, ISBN 1-928589-08-1, (ISBN 13: 978-1-928589-08-2), $16.95

This humanist collection invokes a new vision, one that speaks to readers regardless of their spiritual inclination. "This is an extraordinary book."— John Shelby Spong, author of *Why Christianity Must Change or Die: A Bishop Speaks to Believers in Exile*

Sweet to Burn by Beverly Burch

1st edition, ISBN 1-928589-23-5, (ISBN 13: 978-1-928589-23-5), $15.00

Winner of the 2004 Lambda Literary Award for Lesbian Poetry & Winner of the 2003 Gival Press Poetry Award.
"Novelistic in scope, but packing the emotional intensity of lyric poetry..."— Eloise Klein Healy, author of *Passing*

Tickets to a Closing Play by Janet I. Buck

1st edition, ISBN 1-928589-25-1, (ISBN 13: 978-1-928589-25-9), $15.00

Winner of the 2002 Gival Press Poetry Award.
"...this rich and vibrant collection of poetry [is] not only serious and insightful, but a sheer delight to read."— Jane Butkin Roth, editor, *We Used to Be Wives: Divorce Unveiled Through Poetry*

Wrestling with Wood by Robert L. Giron

3rd edition, ISBN 1-928589-05-7, (ISBN 13: 978-1-928589-05-1), $5.95

A chapbook of impressionist moods and feelings of a long-term relationship which ended in a tragic death. "Nuggets of truth and beauty sprout within our souls."— Teresa Bevin, author of *Havana Split*

Books for Children

Barnyard Buddies I by Pamela Brown; illustrations by Annie H. Hutchins

1st edition, ISBN 1-928589-15-4, (ISBN 13: 978-1-928589-15-0), $16.00

Thirteen stories filled with a cast of creative creatures both engaging and educational. "These stories in this series are delightful. They are wise little fables, and I found them fabulous."
—Robert Morgan, author of *This Rock* and *Gap Creek*

Barnyard Buddies II by Pamela Brown; illustrations by Annie H. Hutchins

1st edition, ISBN 1-928589-21-9, (ISBN 13: 978-1-928589-21-1), $16.00

"Children's literature which emphasizes good character development is a welcome addition to educators' as well as parents' resources."
—Susan McCravy, elementary school teacher

Tina Springs into Summer / Tina se lanza al verano by Teresa Bevin; illustrations by Perfecto Rodriguez

1st edition, ISBN 1-928589-28-6, (ISBN 13: 978-1-928589-28-0), $21.00

Winner of the 2006 Writer's Notes Magazine Book Award—Notable for Young Adult Literature.
"This appealing book with its illustrations can serve as a wonderful learning tool for children in grades 3-6. Bevin clearly understands the thoughts, feelings, and typical behaviors of pre-teen youngsters from multi-cultural urban backgrounds...."
—Dr. Nancy Boyd Webb, Professor of Social Work, author and editor, *Play Therapy for Children in Crisis* and *Mass Trauma and Violence*

www.ingramcontent.com/pod-product-compliance
Lightning Source LLC
LaVergne TN
LVHW050937080826
845145LV00004B/1296

* 9 7 8 1 9 2 8 5 8 9 3 5 8 *